MY FAMILY IS CHANGING
A BOOK ABOUT DIVORCE

Written by

Emily Menendez-Aponte

Illustrated by

Anne FitzGerald

 Publications
1 Hill Drive
St. Meinrad, IN 47577

Text © 2013 Emily Menendez-Aponte
Illustrations © 2013 St. Meinrad Archabbey
Published by Abbey Press Publications
1 Hill Drive
St. Meinrad, Indiana 47577

Library of Congress Catalog Number
2013919777

ISBN 978-0-87029-555-3

Printed in the United States of America.

A Message from the Author
to Parents and Caring Adults

Deciding to divorce is a serious and life-altering decision. It's not one that is made lightly and is even more difficult if you have children. Obviously the decision to divorce will significantly impact children, but with guidance and support they will be much more equipped to navigate this difficult time.

It's best for parents to tell their children of the decision to separate and divorce as soon as it is definite. Even very young children are acutely aware when something is awry. Being honest and upfront about family changes will prevent your child from experiencing the anxiety of imagining a much worse scenario. It's important to encourage your child to ask questions and, just like other conversations you've had, answer as honestly as you can without giving unnecessary details. Developmentally, young children process information at the level of the concrete. Any "extra" information is likely to confuse them more.

This does not mean that even the youngest of children won't have a wide variety of emotions in response to their parents' divorce. Remember that these emotions will most likely be expressed in all types of behaviors. Encourage children to talk about what they are feeling and experiencing. The help of a professional counselor or therapist may be very beneficial in assisting you with this.

All children need and rely on structure, routine, and knowing what to expect next. During the stress of a big life change, such as divorce, these things become even more important. Do your best to maintain routines, structure, and "house rules" as much as possible, even between two separate homes. It is critical that as parents you learn to do this together even though you are no longer a couple. Work to find a way to communicate about parenting decisions. The more you are "on the same page" as parents, the better off your child will be.

Although divorce is a difficult process and monumental life change for children, it is possible for them to get through it and be OK. I hope that reading this book with your child can be a starting point for discussions and explanations of what is happening. Give your child time to adjust—children can be surprisingly resilient. With support, love, cooperation and encouragement, you will be able to help them through.

—*Emily Menendez-Aponte*

What is a divorce?

Mommy and Daddy are getting a divorce. That means they won't be married anymore and they won't live in the same house.

Lots of things will change, but lots of things will be the same, too.

Mommy and Daddy will make sure you know what's going to be different.

It's NOT your fault.

Moms and dads get divorced for lots of different reasons. Maybe they had some loud fights or maybe they hardly talked at all. But no matter why your mom and dad decided to get divorced, it wasn't because of you.
It's NOT your fault.

Sometimes it's just better that parents aren't married to each other anymore.

LOVE

Even though your mom and dad won't be married anymore doesn't mean they love you any less!

Your parents love you so, so, so much. Nothing, not even a divorce, will ever change that.

Both your mommy and daddy will always love you and always take care of you.

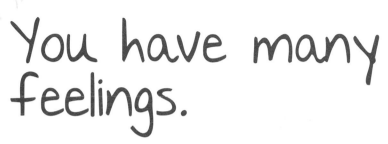

You have many feelings.

You are probably having lots of different kinds of feelings now.

You might be mad or angry, and are maybe very sad too. Maybe you also feel worried and a little scared.

It's OK to feel all these things. Other kids whose parents get a divorce feel all these same kinds of ways. You are not the only one.

Let your feelings out.

It's all right to feel all different ways. What's important is to make sure all those feelings get out of you. Don't stuff them down into yourself. It will make you feel yucky to keep them all inside. Feelings need to come out!

Tell your mom and dad what you are feeling and thinking about.

Talk about your feelings.

Your mom or dad might want you to talk to someone else, like a counselor. Your parents will pick someone they really trust and like. Don't be afraid, counselors talk with kids all the time and are really good at it.

Talking to someone almost always makes you feel better.

Divorce is hard for everyone.

Just like you have lots of different feelings, so will your parents.

You might see your mommy or daddy cry, or be really angry or upset. They might just act kind of strange or different for a while.

Getting a divorce is really hard for your mom and dad too.

Where is God?

No one wants their parents to get divorced. But no one can make sure that doesn't happen. Not you or even God.

But, you can pray to God about things. God wants to help you feel better. God always listens.

It's OK to be different.

Your family will be a little different now, but that's OK.

Kids have all different kinds of families—big families with lots of people or small families with just two people. Some families live together and some live separate from each other.

It really doesn't matter because all families have lots and lots of love. Everyone's family is different, that's what makes them special.

Living in different places.

When parents get divorced they live in different houses. Sometimes moms and dads live close to each other and some live far apart.

You'll probably spend time living with each of them and you'll have special things at each of their houses.

You'll get to see both of them, but exactly when is different for each family. Your mom and dad will work out what's best for you.

This way and that way...

Sometimes you might feel like you are being pulled like a rubber band. It could especially feel like this on special days like holidays and your birthday. This is because both your parents love you and want to be with you.

Your mom and dad will do their best to make things easy and make sure that you are happy. Let them know if you are not feeling good about how things are.

Have fun.

When you are with your mom, you'll have fun. When you are with your dad, you'll be happy. It's OK to have fun and be happy even though both your parents are not there together. They understand this and they want you to feel good.

Your parents don't want you to feel weird or guilty when one of them isn't there. They know that you love each of them very much.

Making new friends.

Your mom or dad might make some new friends. This is normal and OK. Parents like to do fun things too and go out with other adults.

If your mom or dad makes a really special new friend, you might meet them. It might seem kind of strange to see your parents with another person at first. It might help if you can think of at least one thing that you like about your mom or dad's new friend.

Things can and will be OK.

Divorce is really hard for everyone in a family, especially kids. Things will change and be different, but it won't always feel bad. Your mom and dad will help you understand what to expect and what will happen.

The most important thing to remember is that both your mommy and your daddy each love you VERY, VERY much and that will never change, no matter what.

Emily Menendez-Aponte is a licensed clinical social worker and the child of divorced parents herself. She has many years of experience working with all different kinds of families. She is also the author of *When Mom and Dad Divorce* and *A New Baby Is Coming*, also published by Abbey Press. She lives in Connecticut with her husband and three children.

Anne FitzGerald is an internationally known artist and has written and illustrated over 200 children's books. She is creator of "Dear God Kids" and many other children's books and products. Anne works from her studio/gallery in Limerick, Ireland, and teaches art in Liberty Christian School there.

For other books in this series go to:
www.abbeypresspublications.com
and click on "JUST FOR ME BOOKS" in the side bar.